Love's Test

Love's Test

poems
Jed Myers

GRAYSON BOOKS
West Hartford, CT
www.GraysonBooks.com

Love's Test
Copyright © Jed Myers, 2019
Published by Grayson Books
West Hartford, Connecticut

ISBN: 978-1-7335567-1-2

Book & cover design by Cindy Stewart
Cover image © white snow/Shutterstock.com
Author photograph courtesy of Alina Rios

graysonbooks.com

Also by Jed Myers

Books
Watching the Perseids
The Marriage of Space and Time

Chapbooks
The Nameless
Between Dream and Flesh
Dark's Channels

Acknowledgments

I remain grateful to the editors of the publications noted below, where the following poems first appeared:

"Proof"—*Split Rock Review*
"Drowned Man Blues"—*The Delmarva Review*
"Under the Prattle"—*DIAGRAM*
"Mouth"—*The Marriage of Space and Time* (MoonPath Press)
"My Brother's Own Throat"—*Oxford Magazine*
"The Impossible"—*New Southerner*
"Love Poem Written in Broad Darkness"—*Pretty Owl Poetry*
"Two Lights"—The Delmarva Review
"In the Shade by the Water"—*Slippery Elm*
"Night on the Way Back from the Metolius River"—*Cider Press Review*
"Picture Me Beaming"—*Columbia Journal*
"Shadow-Ink"—*Cloudbank*
"Love's Home"—*Broad River Review*
"What I Did"—*The Summerset Review*
"Geometry of the Orbits"—*The Greensboro Review*
"At Last"—*The Adirondack Review*

"My Brother's Own Throat," "The Impossible," "Love Poem Written in Broad Darkness," "In the Shade by the Water," "Night on the Way Back from the Metolius River," "Shadow-Ink," "Love's Home," "What I Did," and "Geometry of the Orbits" also appear in *The Marriage of Space and Time* (MoonPath Press).

Gratitude

I'm very grateful to Ginny Connors of Grayson Books, and to Leslie McGrath who chose this collection on behalf of Grayson Books. Without their welcome these poems would not have found these pages.

I thank Tim Seibles for his greatly encouraging responses at a crucial juncture in the development of this work. Thanks also to Charlene Breedlove for her vision of where my work is going when I can't see ahead. Thanks again and again to my companion, Alina Rios, for her faith and the space she's given me.

And for the making of these poems, my endless thanks goes to all who have tangled and entangled with me in love—all of us timelessly connected through the deepening ordeal of love's test.

JM

This book is dedicated to my children

Isaac, Jonas, and Lily

who have taught me more about love
than anyone or anything else ever could

Contents

Proof	13
Drowned Man Blues	14
Under the Prattle	15
Mouth	16
My Brother's Own Throat	18
The Impossible	19
Love Poem Written in Broad Darkness	21
From What My Brother Could Say	23
Two Lights	24
In the Shade by the Water	25
Night on the Way Back from the Metolius River	26
Steeping	27
Saint Valentine Tours the City	30
Golden Meteor	31
Picture Me Beaming	34
Shadow-Ink	35
Love's Home	37
What I Did	39
Geometry of the Orbits	40
At Last	41
About the Author	43

Proof

Take last night—wasn't much to it—
two earthlings floating our dreams
in one bed. Though it left us

plenty of proof. Didn't we shift
and touch under the dark's one cover,
shuffle our sleeps together

in the gusts of each other's breath,
then slip again deep
into singular drifts? I remember

your forehead against my neck, your arm
on my chest.... You kept
my knee a while between your thighs,

and I roused a little to the wind-
in-the-trees of your inhalations. No
more than this—all the proof

we'd need, to know, throughout
the rest of our lives, we had passed
love's test. And why

doesn't once convince us? As the night
lifted off to its dawn death,
it left us a certain scent—evidence

it had mixed our humors, stirred us
a oneness. Then the light scoured us
separate, our senses'

confluence lost. We showered
and dressed in our doubts—it suggests
we'd learned next to nothing.

Drowned Man Blues

Bitten an apple and halved a worm?
I broke a tooth on a bit of shell slid
in with the oyster.

                    Gone
on a swim, held close to the shore
and thrown under by one pounding
breaker?

        A man I knew drowned
in a foot and a half of surf—hauled
his two kids from the riptide, lay down
spent and was gone.

                        Ever hung
from a limb as it gives? Your weight,
the wind, a blight—how could it
not?

        You have to watch out.
What does the worm know? What
does the sea care if it's for love
you inhale? She'll swallow you whole.

Under the Prattle

God help me, I hide in my skin
disguise. And my words all forgery—
may I not be severely fined.

Lies, filched idioms, rags
tied into kite tails to steady
my rice-paper diamonds in the sky—

all I've provided I've plagiarized.
I'm less real than the gray gull
who openly shatters the shell

to steal the creature inside—I mean
to dangle a morsel, feed you a line
behind your wishes' teeth. For this

am I damned? We're some kind of kin,
and you've left your window open.
Your unfenced garden invites

my trespass. Your trellis incites
my sin. I'll climb in, you unbutton
my herringbone vest, press

your ear to my chest, and listen—
under the prattle out of my lips,
a rumble, a depth, like the ocean's.

Mouth

Little sucker—his mother's nipple
mechanism's jinxed by his thirst.

There is too much need in this house—
she feels eaten. And that old

louse who seeded her, he's out again
late reportedly pleasing the boss

who's got a divorce to talk about. What if
all this life's an insatiable mouth?

she wonders, resting her forehead
against the cold glass of the world

in the bathroom mirror. Little *pisher*—
this mama won't take the call,

cannot let it drag her down
the hall to the railed bed and the piercing

squeal that already explodes in her head.
What if the whole world is one hollow

appeal to be fed? Every one of us
not yet a toddler—pope and president,

every last UN ambassador—it makes her
wish her eyes could exude a few tears,

but bitterness clogs the ducts. Unfortunate
fusser, he knows without thought

he's the big trouble. He'll take a bottle
and she'll go to the kitchen for hers.

Little cur—he'll syphon the most vital
part of her life, his bestial bite

right out of the middle. It will not be
a pleasure. She feels his wail—

the diapered commander has her
hard by her cardiac muscle in his

telekinetic grip, as if
he were still in her, digging

his digits up through her diaphragm
into her left ventricle. Could it be

self after self—one swum out
of the other since conception's own birth,

all from the same subspace lagoon—
tunnels a lineage of the original

urge, and we are the sucking
tubes poking the future, strung out

as long as the sun heats the pool, each of us
hung out to die, a wish out of water?

she muses, eye-to-eye with her silvery
immaterial double. She listens—

a gasp and sigh, a glottal gurgle,
soft exhausted moan of why-bother

out of her caged little *wild animal*,
a surrender, after all, to her

refusal to arrive. Relief
and shame will sink down and dissolve

inside like the droplets of angostura
she'll add to her rye to call it

a cocktail. And she'll drink
to her child, who, when she peeks—

tiny pucker of lips a sign
he dreams he's the fishlike creature

he is in the world's first waters—seems
like a needless angel.

My Brother's Own Throat

Two near-invisible old guys edging
the surf, we amble north, keeping
the constant Atlantic's loud whisper off
to our right with its ledge the horizon.

And to our left, the slow single-file
procession of tall hotels seems endless
as well. We shamble on through
squads of next-to-naked small kids

splashing the shallows. We're in
our clothes. My brother jigs clear
of each frothy fan and keeps dry. I've got
my cloth slip-ons and pant legs soaked.

Gulls, terns, and sandpipers congregate
close, mingled like gangs gotten used
to each other. Human twosomes saunter
beside us in swimsuits. They appear

comfortable so exposed. Their talk
drowns fast in the jostled air.
My brother sputters into the drone
how the last romance spun down

and crashed—around him the stir turns
to the laughter of churned water, children
and birds, and of the chugging
single-prop up there lugging its banner

for a new lotion across the blue span.
And out of my brother's own throat
a guttering tone—he savors the joke,
as if it's on some other old man.

The Impossible

Early May, a cool evening, late
enough in this life I welcome the stray
cottonwood tuft on my jacket sleeve,

loose tangle of fine white hairs
caught on the nap of the light
wool weave. I watch it shiver

there in an imperceptible breeze,
thin airy bundle, sunset-tinted,
stuck for the moment inches

up from my cuff. No bother,
no omen, it doesn't suggest
the least imminence. It's meant

for me as much as the white strip
I'd slip from a crisp fortune cookie.
It hasn't been sent nor found me

an essential stop on its way
to fulfill its fertility, this
weightless fluff seed raft—no news

out of the unseen in its touching
down, nor in how it takes off
just now on a faint gust, gliding

out over the asphalt of 65th
with no eye for the soil, no small wheel
nor rudder, adrift as its countless

blind cousins the snow of the *Populus*
trees clustered a block or so south
by the footbridge above the ravine.

No steerage but wind for the gene-bearing
husks, most never to open
their cores to moist earth, they'll dissolve

back into the world in doorways, gutters,
cracks in the road and sidewalk, stuck
returning to dust with no chance

to unfold. Some have the luck
to settle on spring-wet dirt, uncoil
their code scrolls, sprout, and spread out

their deltoid leaves, to become
the cottonwood trees, shedding their own
bright cotton. By no prophecy,

no keen discernment nor any
deserving, another spring evening,
I was a kite of loose fiber let go

on buffeting currents and scudded
to a weedy loam patch. I took,
and my heart hatched in the ground of this

fortunate madness, love. Here I am
in its deepening shade, where I claim
the impossible—that this will last

longer than the broad cottonwoods stand
in their seasoned slow slow dance.
And all by the catch of a thread.

Love Poem Written in Broad Darkness

I've been advised not to say moon,
not to say heart too often, watch out
for uses of black, deep, or sea,
and never say soul. Don't call the sky
heavens, avoid vast and infinite,
do not apply spirit, don't toss around
love, and leave the flowers out of it.

Desire's a risk, hope hazardous,
and longing best called something else.

So I'm well-warned, no swooner
staring up at that white boat riding
the night. It bears no letter,
no trinket, no tincture sent
to pleasantly jigger my ticker. And no
far shore across that immense water,

no port with a tower tuned
to any of our dazed whimpers.
Our infrared affections unfold
like idiot blooms on loose bony stems
till we end. Our breath leaves no evidence,
no echo off that great body of nothing
but distance. Still, I could call the heights
bruise-blue and you might feel a little
impact, or say I see coal-shine
embedding those promising sparks.

I will say street, as I'm on it.
Shouldn't say solitude but I will,
less alone than minutes ago
in the jostle and slosh of the pub. This
moment I've saved to say love
just once more in this poem, your face
some literal elsewhere, close as ever.

I drift under the halide glare
and, like a fallen dogwood tetrad
crinkled, discolored, missed by the rake,

I scrape along the curb in the draft
of a passing car. Scent of match sulfur
or gunpowder, smell of fatal mistake

in this shaken air, I'm a late idiom
out of place. I'll aim and fire
my antique flare like a brief near star
in your dream-sky. I'll call it a sign.

You'd say it's not there. I'll say my soul did
what it could while there was time.

From What My Brother Could Say

He had to insist till they'd do it,
pull all the tubes. It took them long
minutes, and after, he watched her

mute teeth-baring, her head bent
back on a madly-arched neck,
bleached hair deranged to a froth

her chin jutted up from, the raised bed
like a skyward bowsprit, and an arm
worming above her as if to probe fog.

He stood and stood and the blood drained
out of his head. He sweated. He heard her
gasps grow slower and whine like a rub

against some narrowed resistance
inside. Or it was the syphoning
sound of inhaled air leaving his chest

through the fresh tear in his life.
He left. The hall echoed and clanged.
A nurse came and went. She told him

it was alright, his mother was good
as gone. He thanked her, but says
there are nights her breath hinges on.

Two Lights

You too have seen a bright dot crossing
the teeming night, and known it was not
a star. You'd also have thought

it could be a plane on its great arc between
far-apart cities, or a satellite
caught in its endless orbit. You still might've

let yourself think it an itinerant
star, and watched for it to wander
right into one other point of light,

which itself could've been clustered billions
such solar fires, remote as we are.
If the two lights seemed to touch,

they did not. In a second
they'd part. But it would've meant
what it meant, while, wakeful, you dreamed.

In the Shade by the Water
—*for my daughter*

Our sorrows meet in one shadow, one
stream, like the ravine creek we'd follow
when you were small. I'm back

there in my daydream, your hand in mine
under the tall summer trees, still cool
midday on the path along our little river,

you crouch over slugs, stroke the moss
coats on the earth and alder trunks, talk
silk architecture among the spiders,

squawk with the crows as they laugh
at their own jokes. Eternally cool here
below the sun-cooked bungalows.

Home we'd walk from, it's no more.
I left you, let the screen door swat
the jamb as I strode off alone, years before

you could leave too. Left you in that quiet
cavern, floor bared of my Persian rugs,
fridge groaning its hunger from inside

the kitchen. Over the spent wine bottles,
fruit flies in clouds like ghosts of roses
I'd brought you and Mom. Your welcome

to a new loneliness. I wouldn't let myself
see it then. Now you're across town,
a run-down shared rental, more life in it,

more laughter. You've had me there
once. Here, in the shade by the water
where both our sorrows flow, you step

out of your shoes, as you would, to wade.
I still don't know how to atone.
Your feet slip into the cold on the stones.

Night on the Way Back from the Metolius River

We talked out our blues to the dark,
backs to a log, seated on dirt
the summer'd dried out. Before us
the trees like silhouette curtains parted—
the starry backdrop went back
and back, a oneness of distance

and time, what had cast us all out
on our world lines. We had parked
our families in the motel by the road,
glad for a walk out into the dusk,
chance for a smoke, maybe a tavern's red
sign-glow among the conifer trunks

as we scuffed gravel shoulder around
the long bend. There was no tavern,
but a dirt road to a small lot, someone's
not-yet cabin, and without discussion
we'd sat down for the show. Night,
what can it know? For all the time

it held in its view, it told us nothing—
not how in years we'd be out of our houses,
out of the blame showers, immersed
in the lulls and surges of uncertain touch,
wanderers like when we were young
but old. Could the night have said

there's another road, shown the invisible
need in love's angry bed, turned us
toward not away? I wonder—with all
the star-theater's space before us, for all
our talk of our thwarted urges—what,
if the dark spoke, we'd have heard.

Steeping

Do you
        have to squeal
                out my name

from upstairs
        that crass
                now-or-never

register
     over
          the bannister over

high C
     a needle's
            skipping scratchy

penetrant jingle
          of infancy's
                need blown

open
    and now
            you prednisone-swollen

whale
     my husband
            all the years you were

well
    and you wouldn't
              be the man

I danced with
          our first night
                that Boardwalk

hotel
     between the wars
              you were wonderful

    strong and light
                      on your wingtipped
                                      feet
I was held
        till you turned
                      and clung

to your work
            your mother
                        your mirror

the dimple
          you cinched under
                        each necktie's knot

out the door
          to the train
                    not a kiss you

cry
    after me
            like a tar-beached seal

a gear-stripped
                truck
                      in a mud ditch child

caged
      in a playpen
                hungry and wet

I'm coming
          give me
                    a goddamn minute

I'm steeping
           your tea
                  I'm catching

my breath
        stealing
                a daydream's tail

end
    from back
        near the beginning

Saint Valentine Tours the City

In *my* good name, chocolates and cutesy cards,
Your factory roses bred for that lipstick red,
Your one-night jacked-up dinner prices? Hard
To find out I've sponsored all this from the dead.

I've slipped. I thought my martyr's end was meant
To bless one form of love—embodied souls
Entwined in timelessness—but I've been bent
To plug your sparkling brut and those airy rolls,

White tablecloths, pork sliders at the bars,
Canned serenades and faux flamenco shows.
You call it romance—violins, guitars,
For-hire throats and their wobbly tremolos.

For cut-out hearts and sugar highs I have died—
Your tacky charms, your torch tunes, sanctified.

Golden Meteor

The little fellow I was always wanted
to be getting away with something. Stolen

cigarettes on an old woman's brick patio,
strip of bark torn from a tree. Hiding

the bright red transistor radio under
my pillow, wire along my neck

to the ear Mom wouldn't see when she stepped in
for a last check, I got away

with the Top 40 past 2 AM, silently
singing my harmonies out on a corner

not far from the river, South Street maybe,
tapping a tapered black leather shoe,

snapping my fingers, adding a tenor,
lending my heart to the sound we gave

our desire. Mom never knew
I'd lean into one pinball machine

or another for hours in that ringing room
at the end of the thundering Lanes afternoons

she believed I was studying Hebrew
with Rabbi Goldstein's grown son. I'd flip

the silver ball back out amongst the strobing
islands, practice cursing's essentials

when the ball fell, and get to the synagogue
each time in time for my pick-up. Saturdays

I hopped the bus to the downtown arcades
and even found nudie peeps no one stopped me

slotting my dimes in to play. This grade-school kid
got away with such negatives, self

made of secret defiance, while under
Mrs. McMurray's weekday vigilance

I racked up the As, one ear
on the Settlers' mythic log-cabin ventures

and one cerebral hemisphere plotting
a dance with Shelley to Dion and the Belmonts'

Why must I be-e a teenager in lo-ove?
years before my teens, getting away

with love's thready beginnings behind
the screen of a boy's milk-and-graham-crackers

countenance, behind the scenes of a movie
of smiles and goodnight kisses. Love wasn't

good. I knew it. Love was covert,
it would compose itself of itch and hurt,

would hurtle its long invisible tunnels,
crossing the dark to where it's been summoned,

wearing ash black as a sign of its inverted
charge and hazardousness, till someday

love would emerge naked and utterly
unintended, in its flash out-of-nowhere

way, gotten away off the stable
orbit of the expected, and crash

like a golden meteor smack
in my heart's back yard where I'd planted

and watered my dear disobedience. Dead set
against the correct, steaming, hissing

like an AM radio between stations,
like a hit single 45 rpm

still turning under the needle long after
the song's ended while two kids learn to kiss,

love would broadcast its seething, sound
like the shredding of all our assignments.

Picture Me Beaming

A lit string runs through us.
Sometimes, brighter than day.

Oh, it's aberrant to see it—
a neural fault. Tumor, seizure,
migraine aura....

                      So thin yet
stronger than want or titanium.

Scintillates at frequencies we call
noise in the system. So what

if you don't believe it. Doesn't mean
it isn't. It isn't

what you believe. Listen, the string
sings when our distances pull it

taut. When one of us dying
plucks it. Look. The late sun's
rays streaming through the trees

catch a spider's web and set it
agleam...you hadn't seen a thing.

You twitch this fiber that outlives
all of us when you think *I wish
I could hold her again*,

                      or wonder
How is he now? Write me a letter
Love. Don't lift a finger. Picture me

beaming. Exquisite, that thread's
tug, just then, through the ribs.

Shadow-Ink

You did hold me. It happened
days ago, your arms real
as these arms I wrapped around you,

and on this bed, where the light's been
kept to a trickle by the curtains
I hung for our aloneness of two.

It's quiet as well, which helps
memory fill its several dimensions—
again your scent, intricate

blend of breath and essences,
and your taste, the dissolved
salts of your skin, and the sweat-oiled

friction between our surfaces, and
the vision, smooth plenitude wet
with a splash of predawn lumens.

I keep it this dark and this close
to silence, so I can imagine,
with little distraction, what was,

even from some dreamy perches
alongside where we lay, or suspended
just under the ceiling, or peeking

from outside through the gap
between fabric and sill, to see
the two thrilled glistening people

we were, a morning that might've been
eons ago or a figment. I wish it were
now. How else to be sure?

I want memory to be sufficient.
Its witnesses are with me—sworn
company of the senses. I have

selected a jury. Favorable
angels hover at various angles
to assess recollection's evidence.

Yes, lying here at the scene,
I can decide you've loved me.
It's like seeing it written

with a twig in sand, a breath
before a tide fan sweeps it
away, the shadow-ink spread

in one swipe from the record. When
is it ever enough, to think
of the past? In its absence

doubt is a fast-risen sea—
I am about to inhale it.
Come back. Come hold me.

Love's Home

The body emits. I remember
my mother gathering up the sheets
as I stood by the bed, convinced

I was worse than useless. She hid
her grimace as best she could. Then
there was blood, red ooze at the knee

as I'd done it again, careless, her wince
as she daubed it, cotton wet with Bactine…

and the cries, so often
storming up from the lungs
to force open the grit-gate of teeth….

It's impossible not to emit,
not to press love to its tolerance
limit. How is it

I checked my gag each time as I mopped
my sick kid's chin and chest
again with the rinsed rag?

And wasn't there the elder who fell
as he sat where you'd removed the chair?
Scalp a shell cracked on the floor,

it dripped. You fled—didn't help.
And hadn't a matchbook flared
in the old man's palm, that weeping

crater in flesh a terror, a wish
he'd never touch you with that hand again?

Haven't we each more than once failed
love's test? And as I get old,
I'll emit more, not less—

the whimpers and fluids and breaths
we've dreamed we controlled while it was
chaos taking its time with us—

till it exceeds your threshold, I can't
wash or shower or wipe fresh
any part of myself enough, and you,

young lover, will have had enough,
like my mother, her hour

every two days or so in the chair
in the far corner of my father's last room,

the tumor inside his skull insisting
his body emit every last thing.

Or is there a turn? If you fall
first, is it in me to change
the soaked surgical dressing? Or you might

learn, by love's stubborn duration
alone, this concoction of scents,
this collage of the unhealable

wounds and their seepages, must prove
at last endurable. This is love's home.

What I Did

My hope's a child's. My grandmother
stood over the sink in the summer
morning's south window glow, holding
the rounded box of frozen strawberries
under the faucet's warm rush, her voice
a murmur of pleasure, till she was sure
the insides were thawed enough. Soon,
she'd set the white bowl on the yellow
formica table, the deep red fruit cold,
sliced, ready to lift in the big spoon
from the pool of sweet juice.

                                    This is one
scrap, an age-browned crayoned sheet
tucked in among others—stick-figure
fathers and silvery terriers, thick-outlined
houses, chimneys uncoiling black springs,
smudged tulips, fangs of white fence—
such pages, stuffed in a secret hurry
into the slots between a kid's ribs,
hold up only so well as they're slid
free by these wrinkled hands. See
what I did? Stored the light that poured in
over the rooftops across the alley,
over my grandpop's tomato vines,
in through the kitchen window and lit
my grandmother's cheeks and lips.

                                     Creased
documents coming apart as they open
to my stiff fingers, still, I can taste
the strawberries' smooth and sturdy pieces,
hear the tiny surprises of seeds'
crunch in my lost milk teeth, and savor
that rosy nectar. This creaking body's dark
shelves are crammed with a little fool's
crumbling scrolls of love's promise.
True, false—either way, this knowledge,
her soft hand leaving the bowl.

Geometry of the Orbits

Did we speed up the stars?
Night's over, you've risen—what
can I savor? Those high notes

the birds utter usher a close.
And the crocuses, already gone—
have I shown you one? One

dawn will be the last. The catch
in my throat, a choke on the wind.
We're at the prow of a fast boat.

Or the heart's own sharp minute
hand's clicked past, nicking
the larynx—a little clock joke.

I did kiss the back of your neck.
Its arc belongs to the long
geometry of the orbits—there,

the endlessness. And we are
permitted peeks into the black
behind each other's irises.

At Last

Good now, this bed and you in it,
no hurt in my hip, just the trick
elbow I can't prop myself with,

and I get to hold you and I get
excited like a kid, with fewer nights
left than lived. I can't keep it

under my breath—you'll detect
the grunt-whisper. It presses up
out of my chest, *At last*. I am

embarrassed to expose this interior
nakedness, more than to let you
explore all my faulted skin. *At last*

we've fallen here, out of our pasts,
each had our manic egg-and-seed
dance, our thrash through the marital

bramble, our bitter oak table
settlements, unwitnessed internal
bleeds. Here, the elegant firework

purple allium burst on its long stem
set in a glass flute for you
on the nightstand—faded a little

these few days since it's severed.
The season's advanced. I can't
imagine this blossom replaced.

About the Author

Jed Myers lives in Seattle. He is author of *Watching the Perseids* (Sacramento Poetry Center Book Award), *The Marriage of Space and Time* (MoonPath Press), and three other chapbooks. Recent honors include the *Prime Number Magazine* Award for Poetry, *The Southeast Review*'s Gearhart Poetry Prize, *The Tishman Review*'s Edna St. Vincent Millay Poetry Prize, and the *Iron Horse Literary Review* Chapbook Award. He is Poetry Editor for the journal *Bracken*.

www.ingramcontent.com/pod-product-compliance
Lightning Source LLC
Chambersburg PA
CBHW052045070526
44584CB00018B/2613